MAKING SENSE OF NONSENSE

When Life Doesn't Appear To Make Sense

ADESOLA M. ELEGBEDE

COVENANT PUBLISHING

Making Sense Of Nonsense
When Life Doesn't Appear To Make Sense
Adesola M. Alegbede

Unless otherwise indicated, all scripture quotations are taken from King James Version (KJV) of the Bible.

ISBN 978-1-907734-36-6
First Edition, First Printing June 2018

No part of this publication may be produced, distorted or transmitted in any form or by any means, including photocopying, recording or other electronic or mechanical methods, without the prior written permission of the publisher, or except in the case of brief quotations embodied in critical reviews and certain other non-commercial uses permitted by copyright law.

For permission requests, write to the publisher, addressed "Attention: Permission Coordinator" at the email address:

samadewunmi@btinternet.com

Copyright © June 2018, Adesola M. Elegbede

Cover Design by Covenant Publishing Team
Published by Covenant Publishing
Printed in the United Kingdom

DEDICATION

To the Almighty God and all super-heroes of
faith gone and still living

ACKNOWLEDGEMENTS

To God be the glory for the great things He hath done, most especially for the completion of this book. It can only be God. In hard times, He is my strength. Therefore I recognise, honour, declare, praise, reflect, and live for His glory; because He deserves it.

To my super-hero family, the Truevine Pentecostal C & S Church; most especially the elders and the youth, and particularly Snr Apostle Gbeminiyi Daniel.

To my husband Snr Apostle Akeem Elegbede for his skillful editing of the manuscript. I also appreciate Daddy Adeboyega Talabi for his support, and finally, I am deeply indebted to my beloved children, for their understanding throughout this project.

TABLE OF CONTENTS

Dedication   *iii*
Acknowledgements   *v*
Foreword   *ix*

Introduction   11

1. When God Doesn't Make Sense   15

2. The Perfect Picture   31

3. A Bridge Of Faith   43

4. A Fence Through Faith   55

5. An Anchor Of Faith   63

6. Keeping The Covenant   71

7. A Person Of Significance   81

8. What Really Doesn't Make Sense?   89

Bibliography   95

FOREWORD

One of the greatest apologetic questions that have troubled Christians, non-Christians, philosophers and atheists over the centuries is about the problem of evil. If God is good, why does He allow evil? If He is all-powerful, why doesn't He prevent evil? The main point of this book is that the challenges we face in life will make sense when we choose to understand it from the biblical perspective.

The author, Adesola Elegbede, raised many apologetical questions and sought to answer them in a way that lay men and women will understand. She answered the question by analysing the attributes of God, then reminds us about the sufferings of Christ during His earthly ministry (Mark 14:36). She also touched on the aspect of free will, it's relevance to the topic, and she used many practical examples of past and present real historical situations to drive home her point.

It may appear as if some of the sufferings that humans face in this world are pointless and unnecessary, yet the end result usually brings glory to God. God typically allow some difficult circumstances to bring out the best in us. We can still see His hand in the grand scheme of things which may be for our spiritual maturity or to equip us for ministry. In whatever situation we find ourselves, God is still omnipotent, omniscient and omnibenevolent. As Paul notes, 'the sufferings of this present time are not worthy to be compared with the glory which shall be revealed in us' (Romans 8:18) in the future.

This is a well-written and engaging book which will be of interest to all those who want answers to questions about life or deepen their understanding of the things that appear not to make sense to them.

Rev. Dr G.O. Bakare

INTRODUCTION

Life could not be more meaningless when I lost my precious mum to cancer. I had gone through some life vicissitudes and somehow always weathered the storm (1 Corinthians 10:13). I had a troubled upbringing as a child, had a fair share of matrimonial challenges. The pillar of our economic and financial independence as a family was uprooted at a time we thought we were living justly before God. There is this innate feeling that most humans have; when you are doing the things of God, everything will turn out right! We thought so too! We were wrong.

Moreover, as we continued our sojourn in life, there had been times and things that didn't make sense! Even the Psalmist complained, behold the ungodly prosper in the world, they increase in riches. It does not make sense because the godly toil day and night, they are plagued and chastened every morning.

I had come to know God at a very young age of fourteen through my mum's devotion to God. Indeed, I fell in a trance at one of the revival services she attended in church, and that experience drew me closer to God. My mum taught my siblings and me the way of the Lord. Throughout her sickness, surgery and eventual death, her devotion to God was incredible, and she radiated so much confidence, that "this one too shall pass," having prayed, with other men and women of God interceding for her. Unfortunately, the sickness never passed or so it seemed, but it did not make sense. That she died is not a big deal here – we all will die at some point. The big deal, however, is, it did not make sense to me that despite her complete devotion, prayers and faith, God would still take her under five months when we hear of stories of people, who though not as prayerful and devoted, lived with cancer for years. Some even went on to beat cancer – they got healed!

After that incident, I started to feel some agitations in me. I started to ask questions. Why on earth did God decide to create diseases? Why did he create natural disasters – tornadoes, hurricanes, flood, volcanic eruptions etc.? Why does God allow innocent people to be murdered in terrorists' acts? Why make our world so catastrophic? Why doesn't God take away suffering and pain?

This book is, therefore, a product of my agitations borne out of life vicissitudes. It is now more than ever clear to me that sometimes our lives do not make sense. Nonetheless, you might, in the end, see that there is indeed some sense in the nonsensical things of life. I urge readers that when all hope is lost, when the world seems to be caving in, when all you want to do is lie in your bed and pray to fall asleep instead of falling apart, just remember that, the struggle you see today must develop you for the strength you need tomorrow.

We must realise the fact that, whereas there can be a finite disappointment, but that does not give us the right to lose infinite hope. There can never be a night that would defeat sunrise or hope. Hope empowers one to chase light even inside gross darkness.

MAKING SENSE OF NONSENSE

1

WHEN GOD DOESN'T MAKE SENSE

Maria Kush was barren for forty years, but after several serious prayer and fasting sessions, coupled with attempts to undergo sessions for fertility treatments and administration of various drugs, she was summoned to the clinic by her doctor with the news that she had an ectopic pregnancy, which could result to death if due care was not exercised. She was also told that she must receive treatment as soon as possible. As a believer and a person of faith, she started singing the song "I have a God who never fails" as she was wheeled into the theatre. Tragically, that was the last her darling husband (also of blessed memories), parents and friends would see her. She did not make it out alive!

My mum came back from Canada with loads of gifts for friends and family, with the excitement of wedding bells ringing for her thirty-two-year-old son, but was diagnosed of Jaundice of the Pancreas upon her arrival in Nigeria. Not convinced of this diagnosis, a further test was arranged for her, and it was such an agonising wait for the result to be out. Disappointingly, the result confirmed the earlier diagnosis and added a very bitter verdict – her condition had gone malignant.

However, she remained firm in her faith so much that, even mere looking her in the eyes, one could tell that her "faith will make her whole." Although, from all the medication and laboratory test results, it appeared she was dying, but she held on to her faith and kept echoing the words "I shall not die but live." Looking at her closeness to God, her prayer attitude, her devotion and commitment to God, her service and belief, one would be tempted to say that she would be the last person that God would disappoint or let down.

Does God actually let us down as human beings? Or do we let God down as human beings? We shall attempt to answer these and many more as we dig further into the book. However, the fact remains that, when human beings meet REAL tragedy in life, we tend to react in either of two ways; we either lose hope and fall into self-destructive habits or use that challenge to find our inner strength.

My mum's watch-word in the book of Galatians 6:17 "let no man disturb me, for I bear on my body the marks of Jesus" still holds and was always burning on her lips. Why should God allow her to be disturbed if, for forty-eight years of knowing her as a mum, she never stopped reciting that verse and stood as a role model in faith? She was a staunch worshipper, a believer with very strong energy and hope. She even became a Bible class student at the age of Sixty-eight! Quite naturally, a lot of 'why' would pop-up. Questions such as:

Why not another sickness?
Why not an accident?
Of all ailments, why cancer?
Why not at a later age?

Despite all efforts with prayer and fasting, why couldn't God save her life? Who would judge the universe? For how long should we focus on the brightest when one can find hope in the darkest of days? She lost the battle to Cancer at seventy years of age, a month after she celebrated her birthday and glorified God for keeping her alive!

As for me, the watch-word remains constant. I firmly believe that God has more ropes, ladders and even tunnels out of pits than one can conceive. Therefore, with God, all things are possible. We take consolation in the understanding, belief, conviction, and hope that there is a better afterlife.

A flashback to the Sosoliso plane crash that claimed the life of the Nigerian clergywoman, Pastor Bimbo Odukoya, and to the American pastor that was involved in the plane crash with Dr Miles Monroe and many others, would prompt one to ask, was God sleeping? NO! Even Dr Monroe in his dying moment would agree that "He neither slumbers nor sleep." In the book of Isaiah, He said "my hands are not too short." He will not fail.

What about grace? Does it involve death in a certain way or at a specific time in life? Despite the agonising prayers made for healing by godly people and faithful friends, why should God not listen to their pleas? Does it really make sense?

Despite many such questions God has not yet answered any.

King David spoke about living up to seventy years. Does it mean we should regard ourselves blessed if we live beyond seventy years of age and be ready to die soon after we reach that age? Obviously, No. What of those who died before the age of seventy? Does it mean that God disregarded their request to live longer? What of those who lived above the age of seventy? Was the question answered or not?

In contrast, the word of faith expressed in Psalm 34:19 assured us that "Many are the afflictions of the righteous but the Lord delivereth him out them all." When you hear such word as a person of faith, you feel elated; you feel blessed and happy that all will be well (2 Kings 4:24). However, how can all be well, when it is not well? The Shunammite woman said to Gehazi, hiding the obvious that, "it is well," even when it was not well with her son. In her case, her faith spoke for her; her faith answered to her question, but not in many other people's cases.

Most of the time, God does not make sense, or God does not seem to make any sense. When at first the Shunamite woman's son died, nothing made sense to her. Her son was however revived when Elisha, the man of God, sidestepped Gehazi and laid on the boy for him to regain consciousness. Trying to analyse God's omnipotence is like an Amoeba attempting to comprehend the behaviour of man. Romans 11:33 says "Oh, the depth of the riches both of the wisdom and knowledge of God. How unsearchable are His judgements and His ways past finding out."

The Lord still has not revealed reasons why we must live with evil and where this evil potentially originated from? The life of the foremost Nigerian Pastor, Bimbo Odukoya and those of many that were cut short in several plane crashes makes one question if what God does makes sense. Boko Haram in the Northern part of Nigeria makes one feel sick. How can it make sense for someone to wake up in the morning and realise that all four children she has have been taken by some Jihadist (religious fighters); who in the name of "Allah" could kidnap 300 children (only girls). For more than three years now, Boko Haram has been oppressing and sexually abusing the girls, training them for war and giving them false teachings. How can that make sense to the mothers or parents, who are suddenly deprived of parenthood?

How does one explain the Tsunami disaster of 26th December 2014 where over 230,000 people were killed across 14 countries? A Malaysian Airline Flight 370 took off and suddenly disappeared on 8th March 2014. There were 239 fatalities! Such was also the fate of 228 people onboard an Air France 447 on 1st June 2009. The list is endless!

The way and manner which people are being beheaded in Afghanistan are appalling. The question is, what crime have they committed? All in the name of religion! Could this be the experience of the reality we call 'God'? Why is GOD blamed for everything? What then is the purpose of their tragic loss? It is obvious that almost everyone has one or more questions to ask God. Consider below the repertoire of questions we normally ask when confronted with challenges:

Why me, why me, why me?
Where were you when I was robbed and raped by robbers?
Why did you let my baby die?
Why did you create me a pauper?
Why are you so cruel to me?
Why did you create me to suffer?
Why did you let my marriage fail?
Why am I jobless?
Why am I childless?
Why am I not married?
Why don't you have no beginning?
Why don't you want to answer my prayers?

Do we ever stop to think for once if God has any question for us? If there is, are we at all ready to answer? Has God ever asked us questions at any point in time in our lives? What are our perspectives on this world? Do we blame God for creating us as human beings, or put every blame on Him for the fundamental problems in our lives?

"What literal viability has creation," and "How could mere creatures find it possible to disobey God who had hitherto seemed wholly irresistible?"

In the beginning, God, the first character was introduced as a divine, sovereign being. He loved to fellowship with His creation. God warned Adam, the second character and, Eve, the third character, not to eat from the tree of the knowledge of good and evil, and if they disobeyed, the penalty to follow was "When you eat of it, you will surely die." Adam and Eve were free to eat from any other tree in the garden, save for the restriction God gave them. Both must be tempted on this restriction.

The fourth character was introduced as the serpent. The "ancient serpent" who was said to be craftier than any of the wild animals that God had made. The devil chose to take the form of a snake because he had a spiritual nature (Mark 1:23). He must achieve his aim by taking on the shape of something familiar to his plan. The story is full of enjoyment, pain, anguish, confusion and false starts!

The story of the beginning is an eye opener to man's understanding of who God is, of the creation of the universe, the fall of man, and the curses of mankind which bring anguish into family life. It is a timeless old story that is relevant to the present. It is incredible that we can find such a story that will tell of human generations, the pain experienced in childbirth, the difficulties in the first family which welcome us into the world.

God emphasised His excellence, rightness and wholesomeness of the universe by His pronouncement on each stage of the creation with the word "good." This shows how mighty God is. So how can it make sense that God saw everything that He created as very good yet today, evil continues to exist and even overtake the goodness of His work? How does that make sense? Why is human existence so complex?

About seven years ago, thirty-seven Christians were killed in a massive church hostage. I wonder if any of them had any family or friends that would feel for them or their loss. In 2008, there were series of attacks which were aimed at the Christians in Mosul, Iraq. How does this make sense? On the 9th of April 2017 which was a Palm Sunday, a bomb attack happened and killed at least 44 people. Come to think of it, Iraq was the land where Abraham was born, which was called Babylon in the Bible – where mankind began to read, write, create laws, and live in cities under an organised government!

Today in Iraq, there is a constant slaughtering of people, including children. Natural disasters happen, and no one could give an account of the reason or how it was even caused.

The doctrine of original sin was developed in the early Fifth Century CE by St Augustine announcing the fall of man from complete innocence to long-lasting guilt.

The serpent had been traditionally matched with the devil (Satan) who after he had fallen, turned man against God, but thanks be to Jesus Christ who died on the cross to save mankind from the sin inherited from Adam and Eve's disobedience in Eden.

Could this be the reason why God is not making sense? Come to think of it, has this got anything to do with humanity and its separation from God? Or has this got anything to do with morality? Of course, from the beginning, we were told that God loved and enjoyed fellowshipping with mankind. Therefore, humanity was in total harmony with God and its environment. Little wonder why there was no mention of sickness, hunger, disagreement, pain or death? Now, if there were peace and tranquility in the Garden of Eden, one is tempted to ask, which garden on earth are we in now? Was the then Garden of Eden, the paradise we are now yearning for? Is the Garden of Eden our real home? Is it the unity that God wants with all humanity?

God is the creator of all things. This statement was established in all forms, even in all religious ramifications. God has the ultimate power over His creation. It is a known fact that the knowledge of God must be passed from generation to generation according to His will and purpose.

What about the tree of knowledge of good and evil that was forbidden, and the penalty "when you eat it, you will surely die"? If truly there was death in the tree, then it should not be tasted at all, and that restriction was justified. Does God even make sense here or is God even making sense at all? Many people have taken to the tradition that; the forbidden fruit symbolised a sexual relationship which was consummated without divine permission. Could this stereotype Adam as the cause of evil in the world? The tree of knowledge of good and evil was already in the garden, and the restriction was already given to Adam even before the woman was created. Furthermore, the ban was permanent and not temporary. Therefore, transgression would appear untreatable or incurable since the woman was given to the man to enjoy such a relationship before the fall (Genesis 1:27-28).

In response to this stereotypical statement or notion, sex cannot be a trap for men and women but a gift from God (1 Corinthians 7:4-5). James 1:13 and 1 John 4:8 says that God is love and does not tempt anyone. Is God's judgement truly unreasonable?

There are so many unexplainable sorrows, anguish, pain, difficulty and fear in the world today. Every person must have his or her share and contribute to the explanation of Tornados, poverty, abduction, pirate, untimely death, diseases, bombing, wars, natural disasters and weapons of mass destruction.

If their rational reasoning for the existence of evil on earth or in the world is tied to the unbearable factors which surround Adam and Eve's sin, then what if Adam and Eve did not sin? What would the world be like?

At this juncture and before we get overwhelmed with these questions, let us pause a little and juggle our heads. I think we need an understanding of God; who God is or who made God. Who made the maker of the maker? "God is the supreme spirit Who alone exists of Himself and is infinite in all perfections" (Karen Armstrong). Surprisingly, Karen's definition of God does not make sense to an ordinary man on the street or an atheist. God is that shadowy figure, defined in intellectual abstractions rather than images which remained distant. For most of us that are Christians, our ideas and experience of God had been formed since childhood and still stay on top of the same belief. God is still sovereign and a divine entity. God, is spiritual. He is the creator of the universe. In mainstream Christianity, God is the eternal being Who created and preserves all things.

Prayer Points

- Father, let my delight always be in Your law and give me the grace to continue to meditate on Your word day and night.

- Father, when everything around me seems hopeless and meaningless, let Your word speak meaning to my life.

- Father give me the mind to serve You with fear and rejoice in You with trembling.

- Father, remember me, arise for my sake and let every confusion in my life turn to divine connection.

- Father, help me and kill the power of pollution in my body die in Jesus name.

- Father, let every dream robbers assigned against my life stumble and die in Jesus name.

- Father, Strengthen my hand and let every power that wants me to suffer begin to die in Jesus name.
- Pharaoh of pollution, Goliath of pollution of my father's house, let me go in Jesus name.
- I fire back every arrow of pollution in Jesus name
- Father, let every door of tragedy in my life be shattered to pieces in Jesus name.
- Father, let every stranger in my body begin to fade away in Jesus name.
- Father, let no man prevail against me and let your mercy begin to locate me in Jesus name.
- Father, let every problem coordinators and problem originators in my life disappear in Jesus name.
- Every serpent and scorpion in my family that defeated my parents and wants to defeat me must fail and die in Jesus name.
- Father, let every door of tragedy opened to torment my life be shattered into pieces in Jesus name.
- Father, deal with every satanic addition and subtraction in my life.

- Father, deliver me from strange addictions and attitudes and behaviours in Jesus name.
- Father, disgrace every evil power planning to disgrace me in Jesus name.

MAKING SENSE OF NONSENSE

2

THE PERFECT PICTURE

"But this Man, after he had offered one sacrifice for sins forever, sat down at the right hand of God. For by one offering, He hath perfected forever them that are sanctified" (Hebrews 10: 12-14).

God created man in His image and declared him to be very good. God sees no flaw, spot or imperfection in His creation. However, because of sin, the world became warped and twisted such that imperfections crept in and human desires became self-centred and self-gratifying. In all of these, God still desired to correct man's imperfections and restore him to the original state of perfection at creation

If God created and preserved all things, why then should God allow evil?

The Garden of Eden is a place that God loved to be in; the cool breeze of the evening, walking with human beings, Adam and Eve, fellowshipping with and blessing them. It appeared to be a source of fertility for human being where all resource needed was adequate. It was not clear to Adam and Eve that they were naked and both could not even understand or identify their sexual differences not to talk of knowing the difference between good and evil until they ate from the tree of knowledge of good and evil and literally got their eyes opened. They were able to reason and could choose between good and evil, life and death. This then widened the gap between God and human beings.

The description of God in the Bible portrays God as sovereign (Daniel 4:17-25). If we look at all these attributes, it is evident that God has the power to prevent evil and does not even desire evil for His universe and that He is capable of stopping evil from happening. Why did God even allow evil to happen at all? Why can't God bother not to create evil? Why should evil exist? Why should there be wars? Why should people fall sick? Why sudden death? Why this? Why that? Why is there no logical answer to all these questions?

The ability to choose right from evil is the choice that God gave human beings from creation and if this would cause havoc for human beings, why did God give it? Could God then change everyone's personality so that they would not sin? If this be the case, if the life of humans is programmed by God, if God did not or had not planted the tree of the knowledge of good and evil in the Garden of Eden, if human beings couldn't choose between right and wrong, if human lives were being monopolised by God, being a sovereign God, would all these actions be meaningful? Would there be a meaningful relationship between God and His creation?

Let's get practical a little bit. Should God plan to reverse the act of free will, will it make sense? Would God make sense assuming God wakes us up in the morning and says, man, stand up, go to church, pray, say this in your prayers, do not ask or say more than I tell you, leave church at a particular time, eat at a particular time, you cannot go to work for your work is not serving me, I will give you whomever I want to be your spouse, you cannot have sex with him or her, no sex, no pornography, no partying, no celebration, no stealing, no friends etc. How do you think life would be? What would you do or how would you feel? Does the hypothetical scenario described above make any sense at all?

Freewill (noun), is the power of acting without the constraint of necessity or fate; the ability to act at one's discretion.

If God says no more free will today, what would become of man? Would the absence of free will eliminate evil? Does it mean that evil exists because free will exists? And if there's no free will and there is no evil, would that be God's plan for mankind?

It is so apparent that all the characteristics of God are displayed in God's plan for His people. As a sovereign God, this is demonstrated by the supremacy of God as the creator of "all" things who has the ultimate power to control the universe. But would God even want to be the controller of the universe? Give or take, the eternal nature of God is being experienced by God's people through the means of passing the knowledge of God from generation to generation through teaching and by reciting God's commands. The most common of such in the Hebrew Bible recited to their children is Deuteronomy 6:4 which reads, "Hear ye o Israel, the Lord your God is One, and you must serve Him with all of your might, soul and spirit."

What if they refuse to serve with their soul and spirit? Moreover, if God decides to change His mind, would this result in death? Does the faithfulness of God permit death? Does the free will also come with God's faithfulness or vice versa?

One of the significant characteristics of God is His faithfulness which reflects in His plan for His people by planting the tree of the knowledge of good and evil and by forewarning them not to touch it and also by telling them the consequences. What if man has been faithful to God? Would there be any reason for consequences at all? "If you eat from the tree of knowledge of good and evil, you will surely die".

Was God not fair to have imposed such a restriction? What if God wants human beings to be like Him, act like Him, after all "He made them in His own image". The third characteristic of God explains the distinctive nature of God, which He might have had in plan for all human beings. This shows the difference or the distance between God and unholy or sinful humanity (Exodus 15:11-26; 34:28-36).

Human beings were created and made in God's image, resembling God even in His nature of holiness. If the fruit had not been eaten by Adam and Eve, would human beings have also carried on the nature of God about holiness?

Will it make sense for human beings to have the same sovereign, faithful and holy nature of God?

Many pieces of evidence in the Bible point to the fact that God could, through supernatural intervention, repay human beings their evil deeds, hundred percent of the time! However, if God did this, who would be left in the world?

It may be challenging to controvert the fact that each of us, each day commits one kind of evil or another or unholy act at every point in time. For instance, husband cheating on his wife, wife cheating on husband, drink-drunk driver who because of drunkenness murders by killing, armed robbery, telling lies just to make ends meet, fraudsters, suicide bombers, manipulating customers to gain profit, paedophiles etc. God had chosen to pretend as if all these sins do not count just because if He should begin to count those sins, no one may be spared, meaning that all would be gone. Therefore, He has chosen a real world where as an option, real choices would result in real consequences, which is that real world where we live. Where "the actions of one person affects another person."

Adam chose to sin, and because of this, the entire world lives under the consequence of sin, therefore born with a sinful nature. Moreover, after this, God will come to judge the world of sin and make everything new again, by restoring the world (Romans 5:13). Does it make sense if the result or consequence of man's failure results in the death penalty or curses? What is the aim?

God aimed to preserve life - the first tree that God showed Adam was the tree of life that is everlasting. However, Adam had the choice to eat from any tree in the garden, except the tree of knowledge of good and evil. That was the restriction and thereby a penalty, in case of disobedience to the command "you will surely die." Why would God choose those words, "surely die"? Why not a lesser punishment or just a slap on the wrist? Why would God choose this kind of approach? What was God's motive here, and could this approach be a kind of model that God wanted to use to teach human beings moral ethics? If restriction aims to preserve life, it would then make sense, and God justified!

Life can appear to be cruel to someone who lost his or her entire family in a motor accident or to war. It may seem cruel to someone whose only child died and could not give reasons for the nature of his death. Life will undoubtedly look as if it is cruel to someone who's been expecting or had been through several procedures to get pregnant and at the end of the day, perhaps after several IVF treatments, had a miscarriage and lost the precious pregnancy and not being able to conceive again. Life may appear to be cruel to someone who lost his precious family in a plane crash. Should God be held responsible?

How can God be responsible for all these predicaments, despite His warnings? Would God have allowed all these vicissitudes because human beings or His creation forgot His name or His nature and characteristics or even His being?

He promised not to forget us. Even if our mother or father did, how can He forget the child of His womb? How can God forget His attributes, His loving-kindness, faithfulness, His mercifulness, goodness, greatness, providence and his sovereignty? Why would we think that God will forget His duty to His creation? As the Refuge and the Fortress, the Guide and the One who guards, the Shield to His people or His creation, the One who promised not to leave, forget nor forsake His own; He would not allow His creation to be moved.

God does make sense. If the foundation is destroyed, what can the righteous do (Psalm 11:3)? It is pertinent here to know that there are consequences for everything; be it good or bad. Sometimes, God in His just senses would let a situation not only get bad or worse but get impossible, why?

As human beings see this as the nature of God and for this reason, many things do not make sense even when you are convinced that God is trying to get a new plan for you.

Many of those times when things get so hard, and life gets harder with negative thoughts going through the mind, we do not see God standing even when He is there standing and stretching His hands like a father who is willing and ready to carry his child, no matter the circumstance or situation. Most times we have trouble hearing His voice when such situation arises. We tend to drift away with frustration, disappointment, humiliation and intimidation written all over our faces.

There are many times that what God does, doesn't make sense to us, but we need always to remember that it makes much sense to God. In the sense that, God sees what we do not see, hears what we do not hear, knows the things that we do not know, and understands and knows everything about the universe because He created it. 1 Samuel 16:7 says "But the LORD said unto Samuel, 'Look not on his countenance, or on the height of his stature; because I have refused him: for the LORD seeth not as man seeth; for man looketh on the outward appearance, but the LORD looketh on the heart'" And then the voice of the Lord was heard saying, "Whom shall I send, and who will go for us? Then said I, Here am I; send me" (Isaiah 6:8). Jesus came into the world and was offered as a sacrifice for mankind's sins, and through this singular act, man achieved perfection in Christ.

However, when we look at Jesus, we see the perfect picture of God's attributes. This reflected in His love for His father, His mercy for mankind, and grace to the sinners – never ashamed to dine with them. He also showed us God's holy anger at injustice. These attributes are equally mirrored in human beings through the love parents have for their kids, man's act of kindness and care to the needy and less-privileged.

Also, Jesus mirrored God's perfect attributes in all of His actions. He calmed the storm, demonstrated power and dominion over the earth. He gave freedom to those who were held in bondage. He fed multitudes reflecting God's provision for mankind. Man also reflected some of these, through exercising dominion over other creatures of God; this being the mandate God gave to Adam. Man also enjoyed rest and leisure, and as the Bible records it, God rested on the seventh day, after creation.

Thirdly, Jesus reflects God relationally. In His relationship to the Father, He was showing us what God is like. In His relationship with the disciples, He was mirroring the patience, love (and even frustration) that God has for His children. In His relationship with the blind religious leaders of the day, He reflected God's wrath upon those who tolerate injustice and savour cold-hearted religion. The way Jesus related to the Father, to the disciples, and to others shows us a perfect picture of God.

Fallen humanity also reflects God's image in this way. Even though our relationships are tainted by sin and our relationship with God is often laced with impure motives, the reality of our even having relationships points to the Trinitarian God who made us. We reflect God when we worship Him as Father, Son, and Holy Spirit. We reflect God when we love the people He made in His image. We reflect God when we marry, leaving our family relationships to cleave to our spouse.

Prayer Points

- Father, let Your power begin to resolve every long-term problem and affliction in my life.
- Father, let Your powerful hand perfect everything concerning me in Jesus name.
- All my blessings dedicated to evil powers in the coven must be regained in Jesus name.
- Father, let Your grace abound and be sufficient for me in Jesus name.

- Every chain assigned to tie me down shall be broken into pieces in Jesus name.
- Father, recover for me everything the enemy has stolen from me in Jesus name.
- Every power of reproach tormenting my life must be destroyed in Jesus name.
- Every power assigned to pollute my dreams must be destroyed
- Father, let every problem from the enemy become my stepping stone to greatness in Jesus name.
- Father, let every power of the coven harassing my destiny catch fire in Jesus name.
- Father, declare for me an unstoppable destiny that will confuse my enemies in Jesus name.
- Father, tear apart every satanic lion catching my breakthrough in Jesus name.

3

A BRIDGE OF FAITH

Dictionaries define a bridge as a structure built over a river or chasm to provide a way across. It could also be defined as something intended to reconcile or connect two seemingly incompatible things. One may now ask; why do we require a bridge? Is it God we are connecting to via the bridge? What brought about the nexus between humans and God? How can we connect to God through His way? The Bible says, Jesus is the Way, the Truth and the Life, whoever comes through Him will have eternal life.

In the beginning, man was offered an intimate relationship with God. God said to man, be my friend. God offered man to live in a garden of unparalleled beauty where there was plenty of food, love, intimacy and peace. This offer came on a platter of gold as man did nothing to qualify for this. However, man rebuffed God, through his disobedience. Man said to God, "I do not want your friendship." This, man did by sinning against God. Consequently, this rebellious act of man created a wide gap between man and God. Death also crept into the world as God said that the wages of sin is death. But because of God's love for mankind, He desired that somehow reconciliation should come. Meanwhile, somewhere along the line, an angel appeared to a certain virgin and told her that she would conceive and bear a child whose name shall be called Jesus, the meaning of which is the Saviour. He was to be the one to save His people.

One of the things I studied as a Christian and a student of Theology was the general definition of God and the Christian definition of God. The general definition of God in the monotheistic religions is that God is the creator and the ruler of the universe and the source of all moral authority, the Supreme Being. Practical Christians believe God is made up of three separate beings, that is, the Father, the Son and the Holy Spirit, and they are all one being. How can one see sense in this? There are many different analogies which have been said to explain this concept of the triune God (Trinity). After all efforts to correctly understand the concept, all I was able to get is that God cannot be understood regarding Him continuing to be God unless He is a man.

For many people, the idea of God does not even make sense, in the sense that many things happen to both Christians and non-Christians that are unimaginable. And this can be so disturbing, that one would want to ask the question that, "where is the sense in you believing that God does exist?"

Somebody once asked the question, "Why didn't God stop Myles Munroe's death in the plane crash"? Why did God allow their children to suddenly become orphans? Why Myles Munroe and his wife? Or why should he even die in a plane crash and why did he not die a natural death? I feel the pain anytime the thought crosses my mind and I always ask myself the question, "If I feel this way, how will the children feel? What will their state of mind be remembering the fact that they lost both parents on the same day, at the same time, to such horrific, ugly situation." What if they had been told not to embark on the journey? What of the other people involved? What if they had travelled that journey with their children? What of their positions in the society and their relevance in the environment?

When people are at crossroads, such related questions run through their minds. Somebody once asked why God would allow his mum to die when he was just five years old while another person said he wonders why a God who claims to care so much for His creation, would allow evil to claim people's lives in a war. To many people, anytime a plane crash happens, or a world war or civil war, God does not make sense. However, the fundamental truth is that, in this so-called seemingly nonsensical nature of God, one can find new sense in it. All these ideas make God a complex God, but the complexity of God's nature is indeed the being that God is. There's this saying that goes "Let God be God, let man be man." Furthermore, God Himself says, "My thoughts are different from your thoughts, My ways are different from your ways." God is already God; how? Practically, human being is born on the throne of his own life; we do not even know anything. All we do is fix God into a box which cannot contain him.

Human imagination of God is essential here - the way religion has shaped many of our thoughts. Man, in his wisdom felt by being religious, going to church, doing good and living a good life can bridge the gap between him and God. However, according to Apostle Paul, "It is by grace you have been saved, through faith. Faith in Jesus, not of works lest anyone should boast" (Ephesians 2:8-9). Indeed, all the things regarded as 'good' by man, God calls 'filthy rag' and will not bridge the gap that has been created. We already had the understanding that God is very easy to understand, looking at history and at what the Bible says about God and what is happening in contemporary events. When we look at God's action in the Bible, what the Bible and the teachings we hear most especially in the medieval period, we grew up with the understanding that the world is a flat shape, but after scientific evidence and proofs, we realised that it is round and not flat contrary to the way it looked, Romans 9 says it all.

It is easy for us to determine who we are as human beings but not for us to be able to determine who God is. Why do we expect or believe that we can understand why God allows evil or tragedy or sorrow to happen when we cannot even comprehend the makeup of God? Are we able to figure out why people do the evil things that they do? God sees the bigger picture that we cannot see. Therefore His thoughts are not ours, neither His ways ours, "but as the heavens are higher than the earth, so are my ways and thoughts higher than yours." God has absolute power; He does what pleases Him - the very nature of God is His sovereignty. We were made by God and for God and until we understand that, life will never make sense. If we are going to build a bridge with God, we need to desperately use that method that taps into our genuine desire to please God as Abraham did.

The fact that something does not make sense to one person does not necessarily mean that there's no sense in it. The word sense itself means recognition while Meta-cognition refers to the awareness of ones thought. Sensing itself is already a process; thinking it now depends on the mindset from the perspectives of the five sense faculties in human beings; sight, smell, hearing, taste and touch. Apparently, trying to analyse God's omnipotence is like an amoeba attempting to comprehend the behaviour of man. Luke 1:37 says "For with God nothing is impossible." Is it possible for human beings to live without meaning, without freedom, without being able to satisfy their lust, their identity or justice and hope which represent the ultimate value of life and for me the basis of faith dimension in human life?

Charles Darwin had to take the stand as an unbeliever because of the death of his daughter Annie, which led to the death of his Christian faith. With an eternal perspective, we need to understand that adversity is essential to our internal progression. If FAITH is the bridge between where God is and where you are standing, what then is the position of many and how is it built? Is it like London Bridge falling, or is it like the bridge of the gods in Columbia? How deserted does it seem? After all, faith is the assurance of things hoped for, and the conviction of things not seen, and it goes further that, without faith, you cannot please God.

Making sense out of nonsense

God allowing evil in the world would not even make sense to an ordinary person in the ordinary sense of reasoning. There is no rational or theological explanation for disaster and pain, but the most important thing is to trust God and obey Him (the Biblical narrative). Abraham in the ordinary sense of reasoning would not have listened to God's commandment of him slaughtering his only child and son for that matter, but because of his unfailing love for the Almighty, omnipresent, omnipotent and omniscient God, he did. Let's do a bit of brainstorming here – could Abraham have obeyed because he thought that God might be watching him? After all, God is all-knowing or peradventure God followed him to that place of slaughtering (Mount Moriah), or God already knew that he would obey? (Genesis 22:1-19). It is recorded in the Bible that "By faith, Abraham, when he was tested by God, offered Isaac" (Hebrew 11:17-19). Perhaps Abraham's faith in God is such that God would have resurrected the boy once slain since he had prophesied to him and made a covenant that the boy would be the father of many nations and would be great.

What if Abraham had not complied? How can a sensible, loving God ask that you sacrifice your long-awaited seed, that was born at a ripe old age, even when all hope was lost? Sometimes I reflect on this and try to picture the possible thoughts that might be going through Abraham's mind. Could it be the devil playing his pranks or was it indeed the voice of God? Suffice to ask more questions; does God even tempt His people? Or does God entice His children to do wrong? Or does God test His people? Well, the Bible in James 1:13 has an answer to the questions: it says, "Let no man say when he is tempted, I am tempted of God: for God cannot be tempted with evil, neither tempts He any man."

In Abraham's case, I do not think that God was telling Abraham to do wrong. God has the right to take human life (He created human beings, He gives and takes whenever He wishes – God's moral authority). We need to realise one crucial point here – God commanded Abraham to sacrifice his only son, and he did it of his own volition. Abraham could have refused, and his doing so could have caused him disaster or condemnation by God. (See Saul in 1 Samuel 15:1-35). Saul's disobedience to kill King Agag, the Amalekite king, costs him his kingdom. His refusal to utterly annihilate the Amalekites made God curse him. The point was for Abraham to demonstrate his love and obedience to God, and that he trusted him completely by placing Him above all else – nothing less and nothing else even above his only son! Everything still boils down to faith. To the patriarchs, faith was an experience. To our fathers and forefathers, faith was an inheritance. To us, faith is a convenience, and to our children, faith is a nuisance.

God was to later replicate the action of Abraham by going the extra mile because he did not want humanity separated from him forever, so he sent his only son, Jesus to become man and with a divine assignment take the punishment for our sins. Jesus paid the price for our sins. He became sin for us and died in our place. The fulfilment of this assignment thus made Jesus to be the bridge between man and God. The Bible in the book of Romans says, "At just the right time, when we were still powerless, Christ died for the ungodly. Very rarely will anyone die for a righteous man, though for a good man, someone might possibly dare to die. But God demonstrates His own love for us in this: While we were still sinners, Christ died for us."

God always show that He is making sense out of nonsense by asking us to prove our love or faith or trust in Him through our actions. James 2:22 says your faith can only be made complete by what you do. Abraham's faith was made complete by what he did! 'For God so loved the world, that He gave His only begotten Son, that whosoever believes in Him shall not perish but have eternal life" (John 3:16). Meaning, the death of Jesus Christ on the cross is a night mere for those who cannot believe or fathom it, how can a father allow his only begotten son to be brutalised and murdered in such a despicable manner just because he must save mankind?

Even some of the monotheistic religious groups will throw up their spittle and receive it with their face, or be ready to kill if you dare mention Christ as God or the Son of God. To them, it can never make sense! What then will make sense to such people is quoting John 1:2 "In the beginning was the word, and the word was with God, and the word was God," since the Quran testifies to it that Jesus is the word of God. Why does God even want to test His children? James 1:12 says the testing of our faith comes from our father who works all things together for the good of those who love Him. Abraham believed God, and it was counted to him as righteousness.

Hebrews 11:13-16 says "These all died in faith, not having received the promises, but having seen them afar off were assured of them, embraced them and confessed that they were strangers and pilgrims on earth, for those who say such things declare plainly that they seek a homeland, and truly if they had called, to mind that country from which they had come out, they would have had opportunity to return, but now they desire a better, that is, a heavenly country, therefore, God is not ashamed to be called their God, for he has prepared a city for them."

"Let us hold fast the profession of our faith without wavering, for he is faithful that promised" (Hebrews 10:23). Christ stands as the object of our faith (John 3:36). For obviously, if there will be any efficacy, our faith must rest in Him alone.

Prayer Points

- Father, cast me not away from thy presence, take not Your Holy Spirit from me in Jesus name.

- Father, let me see light in Thy sight and continue Thy lovingkindness with me in Jesus name.

- Father, remove thy stroke away from me and spare my life in Jesus name.

- Father do not let my strength fail me in Jesus name.

- Heal me and let me be healed, save me and let me be saved through the blood of Jesus.

- Balm of Gilead, heal all my afflictions and diseases with the power of the Holy Ghost.

- Powers injecting me at night must fall and die in Jesus name.

- Father, deliver me not into the will of my enemy and save me with your right hand in Jesus name.

- I breathe in the fire of the Holy Ghost and breath out all afflictions with the fire of Elijah in Jesus name.

- Father, let positive angels begin to bombard my life with blessing and glory in Jesus name.

- Father, let the wickedness of the wicked in my life come to an end in Jesus name.

- Father, let the power of infirmity and generational ailment in my life fail in Jesus name.

- Father, every stranger assigned against my body begin to die in Jesus name.

- Father, let every owner of evil load, inform of sickness, affliction, diseases, infirmity, sorrow, shame, poverty, barrenness, joblessness, begin to carry their load in Jesus name.

4

A FENCE THROUGH FAITH

The last time I checked the dictionary about the definition of the word 'test', it said a procedure intended to establish the quality, performance or reliability of something especially before it is taken into widespread use. Could test and trial have the same or similar meaning? 'Trial' is defined as a formal examination of evidence by a judge or a test of the performance, qualities or suitability of someone or something. On the contrary, 'temptation' is defined as the desire to do something especially wrong or unwise. Why would God test His children? Why should He? Is testing even necessary? God's test is to ascertain our faith in Him or for a continuous assessment to confirm our trust in Him. Was Adam tested by God's instruction of the forbidden fruit? Why should the problem of evil be linked to Adam's and Eve's disobedience? Why do we see God's actions as sometimes not making sense? The wall has been brought down and needs to be raised up. How do we build fences with God through faith?

Satan was initially a perfect angel but refused to stand fast in the truth (John 8:44). Because of his desire to covet that which rightly belonged to God, he failed woefully and fell. Eve was persuaded by Satan to obey him instead of God, therefore disobeying God. Adam was persuaded by his heart, his loving wife Eve and that decision led to suffering and death. In a nutshell, Satan was and is still today rebelling against the sovereignty of or the position of the Most High God and mankind have followed suit.

The forbidden fruit was not placed in the garden to test humanity but to prove the sovereignty of God. Satan has become the ruler of the world, and the majority of mankind have knowingly or unknowingly joined him (1 John 5:19). Satan tempted Jesus to jump off the pinnacle of the temple if indeed He is the Son of God, just to display His faith. God intended humanity to have the freedom to express their love for Him. Everything that God made was perfect including His angels. God created human beings with the notion of choosing between good and evil. The only way mankind can indicate this choice is by his doings. Faith has to be active, not passive.

'Test' in Scripture means to prove by trial, and so when it seems that God is not making sense and we get exhausted by His tests on us, the only purpose is to prove that the faith we have in Him is real. God says in 1 Corinthians 10:13 that he will not test us above what we can bear. What about Job? For people like Job, testing is just an irritation, but for others, it is affliction or attack from Satan. Some people produce positive results from testing, and others produce negative results.

One would understand correctly that as devoted as Job was, the reason for his suffering and trials was for God to see if his faith could be broken and if he would eventually curse God. By God's standard, Job was a devoted man. What God did to Job was something that seemed as though was unfair and contrary to what God does for His followers. How could God allow Job to suffer?

I struggle with some "why" also; why did God allow my mother to suffer and die in her sickness? Of all ailments, why cancer? Why make it a short-term disease? After all, we see many who have cancer for several years and still live. She was an epitome of complete faith. She was the last person one would have wished death for at Ninety, not to even talk of seventy! How can someone who had undergone an operation decades before and came out with the thyroid ailment, then fibroid and overcame all these, lose the battle to cancer? However, there's a lesson in her death like in Job's case.

As human beings, we need to understand that things do not operate through human standards or logic. God's wisdom, love and understanding goes beyond humans, and His actions towards humans are a result of His divine character. Of course, human reasoning and nature will always question God's actions, and that is why God's response to Job was "Where were you when I created the world?" (Job 38:4). We are limited in perspective as humans but notwithstanding, our observations may still help us in some extent, to see God's purpose in His actions towards Job or towards my mum, or towards our predicaments.

There are many lessons in the story of Job. God might be using Job's suffering to teach his wife and friends, the reality of life encounters. Also, it might jolly well be that God was using the suffering as a narrative to teach us that suffering can be recorded with laughter and joy. It is important to note that lessons about suffering in the human condition are part of life - God's plan for humanity. Job still did not die in his suffering, so why do some die in their trials and suffering? Is it tragedy or destiny? Why did the Creator even include suffering and death? Is God too weak to prevent suffering or weakness, despite being regarded as sovereign? Is God cruel or vindictive? Is God responsible for human suffering?

Growing up, I was fed with the story of Tai Solarin, a renowned Nigerian Educationist, who refused to believe in God's existence because of his twin sister's illness. While on her sick bed, he begged God to intervene, but the sickness eventually claimed her life and consequently, he decided God did not exist. There are still people like that on earth. Such people battle with hope, trust and faith. "Faith is the substance of things hoped for and the conviction of things not seen," which to a layman, will make no meaning in the ordinary sense of it, but in the spiritual sense, it is a standard statement of Christian faith. "Without faith, it is impossible to please God" (Hebrews 11:6).

Faith can move a mountain if we desire. "So Jesus answered and said to them, "Have faith in God. For assuredly, I say to you, whoever says to this mountain, 'Be removed and be cast into the sea,' and does not doubt in his heart, but believes that those things he says will be done, he will have whatever he says. 24 Therefore I say to you, whatever things you ask when you pray, believe that you receive them, and you will have them" (Mark 11:22-24). How then do you become relevant in an ever-changing world?

No matter the amount of staunch one tries to pull with God, faith puts one in the light, illuminates, empowers and strengthens. Faith justifies us as it did to Abraham. The real test of faith is the strength we display in times of trouble that makes us seem like a superhero and that is what God aims for, whenever He tests us. Testing is also a tool God uses to shape our lives or to correct us. What God demands from us is endurance. God wants us to rely on Him. Therefore, empowers us to bear or endure the situation, which is the key to our promotion from a dimension to another. It even helps our faith to withstand the test of time. Whoever endures to the end shall be given the crown of glory, for Christ is the hope of glory.

Prayer Points

- Father, recreate my destiny by the power in the blood of Jesus.

- Father, illuminate my heart with the sound of heaven in Jesus name.

- Father, by the reason of the anointing, break every yoke in my life in Jesus name.

- Father, turn thyself to me and remember me for good in Jesus name.
- Father, let Your power of discernment and the anointing of fire begin to locate me in Jesus name.
- Father, let Your fire from heaven incubate my life in Jesus name.
- Father, visit me with supernatural power in Jesus name.
- Father, let every flying wickedness in my heaven begin to fall down and die in Jesus name.
- Father, let the wings of every flying wicked in my life begin to catch fire in Jesus name.
- Blood of Jesus arise in your power and scatter every form of wickedness above my head in Jesus name.
- Let the power of God begin to move every movable, shake every shakable power of the enemy against my life in Jesus name.
- Deliver me oh Lord from bloodguiltiness in Jesus name.
- Let me see my desire upon my enemies in Jesus name.

- Make haste to deliver me and make haste to help me Lord
- Father, let the earth yield her increase for me Lord.

5

AN ANCHOR OF FAITH

In the beginning, God saw everything He created and behold, it was good (Genesis 1:31). Everything God created was good, without defect, without blemish. Faith beyond measure is the result of finding Christ in the scriptures, from Genesis to Revelation.

Adam and Eve were perfect; there was no to kill animals to get food. No need for animals to prey on each other. The originality of God's idea of creation was endowed with beauty, a beautiful place as the Garden of Eden, which was full of life, full of joy and reigned with peace in the presence of the Creator of the universe (Genesis 1:29-30). The passage states clearly that God gave Adam and Eve and even the animals, plants and fruits to eat but, about 1,600 years after the flood, during Noah's period, man began to eat meat (Genesis 9:3).

Obviously, the Bible gave us the distinction that death was never part of God's initial plan in creation and was confirmed in Deuteronomy 32:4 that everything God made was perfect. What then makes the difference? What happened that changed God's plan for creation? Romans 5:12 states that "with the rebellious actions of one man, death entered into God's creation."

Adam and Eve covered themselves with fig leaves, but God killed an animal and made a skincoat for them to cover their shame. That is the lamb that was slain – Christ (Revelation 13:8). Why should this affect all human beings? According to Romans 3:23 "For all have sinned and come short of the glory of God." Therefore, when the first man and woman sinned, God cursed the universe and this in effect changed God's plan (Romans 8:22). As said earlier, trying to analyse God's omnipotence feels like an amoeba trying to comprehend the behaviour of man.

To help our understanding at this juncture, I want to implore my readers to see things from a spiritual perspective. For a clear understanding or clarity of the nature of God, one must be spiritually minded or else you are like a blind man. To be spiritually minded is life but to be carnally minded is death (Romans 8:6).

Remember, Jesus deliberately spoke in parable (Matthew 13:11-15). It may appear or sound like mysteries to you, and you may find yourself asking questions like how does this concern me? Why should it affect my parents? However, by the time we begin to see it in the spiritual sense, you will understand.

God asked Job if he was there when He created the universe. In Job 38:4, we read, "Where were you when I created the world?" Obviously, Job was not there when the worlds were created; even we were not born then. Was there any sin involved directly by Job (Job 1:22)? No. The fact is, Job needed some strength here. After all, God is our strength and refuge. The sad thing is what is confirmed in Romans 8:22. Therefore all human beings must suffer from the effects of sin caused by the first man and woman, Adam and Eve. Many faith patriarchs and God worshippers went through similar ordeals, and testing, but faith apparently happens to be the only way out to please God and, the only object one can be tested through, and to trust in for salvation.

In Job's case, God had to prove to Satan that Job indeed was a man that was perfect and righteous. That could be your case. His faith was tested beyond imagination yet did not cause his death. In the case of Abraham, his faith had to be tested for him to be called a righteous man.

Joseph went through injustice, betrayal and temptation, despite his complete devotion to God (Genesis 50:20). Ruth was a virtuous woman who left everything for a higher purpose (Ruth 1:16-18). Esther went through her ordeal but seized the day not just for her people but also for God (Esther 4:4).

Shadrach, Meshach and Abed-Nego were tortured and humiliated in the burning furnace until 'fire turned into air-condition' and the three felt the presence of God and what seemed not to be making sense appeared to be sensible. God decided to show up and save them from the horrors of the fire.

Daniel must either denounce his faith in the Almighty God or be thrown into the lion's den to be devoured. Probably one of his reasons for not giving up hope is because, for him, everything is hopeless. The fact that the Jews were in captivity already was frustrating enough, and if anything will make sense here, it then means that Daniel would go on his knees, damn the consequence, and ask God for help in the open for the lion to become Daniel's friend within the twenty-four hours of trial and terror. Eventually, Daniel was rescued by God by shutting the lion's mouth.

Elijah, the great prophet of fire, faced strong prophets of Baal, men in the world of darkness and wickedness, but stood still and waited for God's ultimate reaction that seemed hopeless while it tarried. The whole scenario was not going to make sense even as the water turned into fuel and burned the whole of the sacrifice to prove God's omnipotence.

All those mentioned were rescued, but a lot were not, and yet they served the same God. They suffered hardships for their faith. They were beaten, battered and bruised. Some of them even died in the process but still did not deny or compromise their faith (Hebrews 11). Some died in their hope - those who were killed because of their testimony for Jesus were called Christian martyrs. This occurred in the early church years through either torture, stoning, burning at the stake, or crucifixion. The word martyr is a Greek word meaning witness or testimony. Where was God then, when Stephen was stoned to death (Acts 6:11:13)? Stephen happened to be the first Christian martyr after Christ Himself. Because he spoke the truth about Jesus Christ, people got offended by his testimonies and therefore, stoned him to death.

Andrew, who was previously one of the disciples of John the Baptist, and also the brother of Simeon Peter, the founder of the church in Byzantium or Constantinople, was crucified on an X-shaped cross because he refused to be crucified the same way as Christ for the mere reason that he felt he was not worthy.

Simeon Peter, the founder of the church in Antioch was also crucified upside down because he also refused to be crucified in the same manner as Christ.

Many people in the early centuries were also martyred and became witnesses to their faith, in the likes of Polycarp who was an apostle of John. John Wycliffe known as the morning star and also a 14th-century Theologian was persecuted and suffered a stroke while saying Mass in a church parish. John Huss, a Czech priest, was burned at the stake for heresy against the doctrines of the Catholic Church. William Tyndale, a reformer who translated the Bible into English was choked to death while tied to the stake, and his dead body was burnt.

Paul, the apostle, was so passionate in his belief that he would not even mind walking on broken glass to win people's heart to God. Paul was so fervent in his faith that, he was not just ready to be imprisoned but was ready to die. Paul would be ready to convince the likes of King Agrippa including the Pharisees, the Sadducees, the Greeks and even the Jews that Jesus Christ is the Son of God and the Messiah. He was sacrificed for his faith.

Where was God when Paul was going through his travails? Was God silent? Was God absent? Why did God choose to keep silent? Paul once asked God three times to remove the thorn in his flesh, but God said His grace was sufficient for him (2 Corinthians 12:7-9).

Why the seeming inaction? Does this make sense at all?

Prayer Points

- I draw the battle line today with the blood of Jesus.
- Father, bless me with faith that will move mountains in Jesus name.
- Father, let my testimony today, be the beginning of unending laughter in Jesus name.
- I shall rise up and not be few in Jesus name.
- Father, make me the poison the enemy cannot swallow in Jesus name.
- Father, let the blood of Jesus clear every sin of affliction arising from my foundation.
- Every power harassing my health, I single you out with the blood of Jesus.

- I come against every power of the coven swallowing my virtues, vomit them by fire in Jesus name.

- By the power that dried the river of Jordan, every river of generational curses in my life must dry up in my life.

- The door that no man can shut must begin to open for me in Jesus name.

- Power of untimely death must lose its hold upon my life in Jesus name.

- Any power that hates my existence is rebuked and destroyed with the power of the Holy Ghost in Jesus name.

- Every power monitoring me for evil must be destroyed with the fire of the Holy Ghost.

- Every dark covering upon my life must catch fire in Jesus name.

- I declare that there shall be no loss of life, property, possession for me and my household in Jesus name.

6

KEEPING THE COVENANT

When God is silent, when we feel the heat, when all hopes are dead, when God is not speaking, when one is helpless, how does one maintaining his faith at this crucial period? How do we continue to play our part in the covenant with God without flaw? What is your conviction that God is at work? All indication from the scriptures, confirms that, He who keeps us neither slumbers nor sleep. It is a known fact that God does speak through His plans, even when you think He is silent, the end justifies the means. "My covenant will I not break, nor alter the things that are gone out of My lips" (Psalm 89:34). God does not meet our expectations but exceeds them, albeit in ways that seem incomprehensible!

It is very pertinent to remember that, Christ died even before all those martyrs stated earlier. If then we are puzzled about the fact that, these people do the things of God, and yet, a lot of things still didn't turn out right for them, and we ask questions concerning them, what sort of questions would we then ask concerning Christ who was His Son?

While suspended on the cross of cavalry, Christ Himself asked God this very profound question, "My God, My God, why has Thou forsaken Me" (Matthew27:46)? What answer was He given? Did God keep silent? Was He asking that question for his own sake? Would God abandon His own Son to the mockery, shame, horror and suffering of the cross? It is so easy to forget God's presence and power when we face uncertainties and tough times. As our faith falters, we doubt that God's presence is real. Hebrews 11:13 quotes, "All these died in their faith not having received the promises but having seen them afar off." This explains the reason why Paul would die defending his faith and said he was content in all circumstances. Little wonder then he said he is not ashamed of the Gospel.

Christ was made a sacrifice, for cursed is he that is hanged on the tree, that the blessing of Abraham would come upon the Gentiles. If this also explains why God did allow His own beloved Son to be crucified, why then did God not forgive humanity without human sacrifices?

Reconciling love and death is such an awkward thing to do. An ordinary person who has no iota of knowledge of Christianity or faith in God would see these two words as contradicting which does disprove the concept of a loving God.

It will break any parent's heart to watch their child being brutally beaten, suffer and die, but, the fact remains that, God consciously decided to send His Son to earth with the knowledge of what would happen because of the love He has for His creature, so that he can enjoy full relationship with God in His presence. It feels so painful when we lose someone who is dear to us, but Christ knowing full well the implication of His action, willingly laid down His own life to separate human being from becoming slave to sin. The reason being that physical death is the only means by which the spirit of people can enter directly into His heavenly presence. Would that be His reason for someone in such dilemma? Why then does God keep silent? Why does it seem that God has changed His address? It appears as if God has disappeared from one's life, and it seems that God is not keeping His covenant, or He has broken His covenant.

A covenant is an agreement between two people or a contractual deed between God and His people. God makes promises to His people and typically requires them to play their part, and carry out their responsibilities. Because it is unilateral, God offers it, and human beings are called to accept it, "For he is not a man that would lie or son of man that will repent." God has never broken His covenant with humanity. Even after the fall, God still graciously maintained His mandate, restored human beings to fellowship with Him, and pronounced the assurance that, the woman's seed would have victory over Satan and his seed. Therefore, the covenant of grace was established.

One of the reasons why we believe that the world is round is based on authoritative scientific revelation and other speculations while, on the contrary, if one could trust one's perceptions, the world would appear as not round but flat. In the real sense of it, as human beings, our situation always determine how we experience God. Therefore, God's silence or absence or distance is such an experience that is too phenomenological!

The same way we see the world that it is flat or round, is the same way we experience God when He is distant, or absent or even present. Obviously, it is certain that the experience of God remains a mystery. How does one explain the fact that through one man, sin came into the world and through one man that is made a sacrifice, we will not die in sin? Are we trying to underestimate the effect of our sins? Is God then silent because of our sins? After all, the face of the sinner cannot behold Him. Perhaps, God is disciplining us for a purpose, or He is testing us so He can promote us (Hebrews 12:10). As the saying goes "He stretches us to promote us." After all, problems are opportunities for the skilled. Therefore, we tend to grow more in faith during hard times.

When it feels like God is not close by, the heart grows fonder, always seeking God. You feel alone, disconnected, hopeless and unworthy when God seems far from you. On the contrary, when God is near, and everything seems excellent and smooth, there is the possibility that He may be taken for granted and the familiarity will breed contempt. In this case, we get carried away, get distracted, wear the garment of disobedience and pride thinking that we can be saved by the multitude of our chariots.

According to Bloom (2014), imagine "if desire is to earth, then, what is sight to heaven?" The desert always awakens and sustains desire. God uses the desert to dry up human being's infatuation with worldliness, which as a result, draws us to the thirst and the well of the coming world.

It is human nature to praise God when the going is good, but many times when the going is tough, we get bitter instead of better, we get negative instead of positive, we get discouraged instead of encouraged, we get pessimistic instead of being optimistic, and we hold on to resentment instead of reconciling. We believe that the thirst, desperation, frustration, and deprivation is a punishment from God, hence His silence.

Why should riches, ease, wealth, abundance or prosperity produce the worst character in human beings, whereas, the best character in us is produced out of suffering, scarcity, deprivation and hardship? Does our humility in times of depravity make any sense? According to Martin Luther King Jr, "The ultimate measure of a man is not where he stands in moments of comfort and convenience, but where he stands during times of challenge and controversy." An analogy of human travails and triumphs is found in the Rose and the Thorn. Roses are lovely and sought after, their colours and the natural scent, which oozes out of them, are enchanting. No wonder, people use them as expressions, symbols or tokens of love. However, a fresh rose that is not pruned is deadly because of its sharp, deadly thorns.

When God is silent, God is working either with time or by time. God is a Spirit Being Who has no physical composition (John 4:24). God is invisible to human sight. The belief in a self-existent God is primary truth; God is never given any sort of physical description. God is Spirit, those who worship God must worship in spirit and truth. God is most glorified in us when we are most satisfied in Him.

The most pleasant thing about God's silence is that the stillness in His silence is very contagious, in that there comes an inaudible voice that entraps and engages you. It gets to the point that you will be forced to listen even when you think God is not speaking. The silence in His voice is louder than the roaring in a fool's voice. Psalm 46:10 says "Be still and know that I am God." The stillness is very important, and it appears God has proven His sovereignty. When you know the word of God, you know the character of God. Even a fool, when he keeps silent is considered wise, when he closes his lips, he is considered prudent (Proverbs 17:28). God's silence is proof of the first sign of the intimacy of God, and it is to stretch us, empower us and also to deposit confidence in us.

As His Creation, God does not owe us any explanation. What if He had explained to Job His actual plan? In human perspective, we tend to believe that if God tells us the reason for our impending suffering, then we can justify and be able to bear it. Could that be possible? God asked Job, "Did you ever ask how the world came into being?" Job could not even figure it out because we mortals are limited in perspective, experience and understanding. Therefore, during those periods that we are pushed to the wall and it seems nothing is making sense around us, when God doesn't seem to make sense, it means we are also players in a cosmic confrontation. According to ancient history, we are privy to that deal made between the Creator and Satan. Therefore, our faith matters.

We need to start making sense of God since we are not privileged to see His hidden purposes for our lives. We need criteria for us to determine if our desires match the abilities we possess. The truth about life is that danger is real, and fear is a choice, but greatness is at the end of destruction. God's plan is always the best. Even if the process is painful and hard, we still need to recognise that, when God is silent, He is doing something for us.

Prayer Points

- Father, cancel every evil covenant arising from my generation with the blood of Jesus.

- Father, convert every issued curse against my life into blessing by the blood of Jesus.

- Father, let the blood of Jesus begin to erase every evil enchantment and divination arising from my generation in Jesus name.
- Covenant keeping God, arise and beautify my destiny in Jesus name.
- Every Goliath spirit from my maternal and paternal family must be destroyed by the power of the Holy Ghost.
- Father, let the anointing upon my head speak against failure in Jesus name.
- Father cut of every strange man and woman in my dream in Jesus name.
- Every demotion yoke downgrading my life must catch fire in Jesus name.
- I bury today every principality assigned against my breakthrough in Jesus name.
- Every agenda of Satan against my life will not prosper in Jesus name.
- No weapon fashioned against me shall prosper in Jesus name.
- Every idol swallowing my virtue must vomit them and die in Jesus name.
- Every occultic agent chanting my name for evil must die in my place in Jesus name.

- Any power of the enemy arresting my foreign benefit must be destroyed in Jesus name.
- Every power blocking my forward movement must clear away in Jesus name.
- Witchcraft vipers assigned against my glory must die in Jesus name.

7

A PERSON OF SIGNIFICANCE

Challenges are not meant for the irrelevant in the society. You cannot be noticed if nothing about you is significant. The question God first challenged Satan with was "Have you NOTICED Job?" Satan would never take anything for granted but always find fault. It is like putting too much salt in a pot of stew. Trying to show off Job puts his life in a mess!

God holds His children with a high degree of importance, therefore, put His children in the position of dominion from creation and not under dominion. "Let us make man in our image, in our likeness and let them have dominion over all that is created" (Genesis 1:26). For that staff of leadership placed upon human shoulders, God is always ready to showcase His own, not minding what the devil or anyone thinks. God is not a man that should lie or the son of man that would relent, or pretend; He has never been stupid or shy.

It has been established that the most consistent debate about God and His existence is the discussion on the problem of evil and suffering, but, by the time we put together everything God has done and still doing, then one's identity with Christ will be vividly recalled. Christ's theology is such that indulges an interrogative faith. The scene started with the face of a baby, who later grew up, ate, drank, taught, preached the kingdom of God, healed the sick, was transfigured, prayed on the mountains, prayed in Gethsemane, washed the feet of His disciples, kissed by Judas, then got arrested, was tried, flogged, dragged, crucified, rose from the dead and ascended into heaven, and thereby, became the hope for the world.

What it means to be relevant is doing what is appropriate as Christ did. To face Jesus Christ means learning to be responsible before Him, learning to be judged by Him, to look on others as Christ looks on them, to be vigilant, responsible, to speak and be silent in His spirit and to be open to radical surprise, bringing glory to God.

Come to think of it; all Job did wrong was that he was a righteous, faithful and fearful individual, blessed with wealth and possession.

The story then changed when God asked for the accuser's opinion of Job's piety. What sense does it make for God to be asking the devil about His own being? Would there be any relevance in that from a human perspective? Whenever we want to address the problem of theodicy, that is, the vindication of the justice of God in the light of human suffering, we usually do have different perspectives. Therefore Satan's own perspective of Job was that Job was good to God because of his relevance in the society. How could God be so callous, mean, and terrible to have allowed that so-called Satan to strip Job, ravage him and kill his ten children? Could it be that all Job had, including his ten children, were taken away in a twinkle of an eye because God wanted to test him? He was even inflicted with painful sores - what an extreme situation!

Let's do some arithmetic. It usually takes nine pregnancy months before the birth of a child. Hence Job had a loss of ten multiples of nine months, which equals ninety months, to start with. The ten children were not babies, not teenagers, youngsters, but adults. Consequently, his loss would have increased by the time we add their different ages! What could be more painful or shattering? But come to think of it, Job could not have been relevant in the sight of his accuser if God had not allowed this to happen to him.

Would you blame Job's wife for telling him to curse God and die? How can Job become relevant to his wife if she never told him to curse God and die? His vintage answer to her was another question, "shall we receive good from God and not receive evil?" What is the sense in Job's question?

The narrative of Job is compelling but still a relevant tale even to its contemporaries. The ordeal is such that poses some significant questions for the faith of believers in all ages and time-honoured classic story and analysis. Job represents us all in our encounters and predicaments with struggles, suffering, sorrow, pain, social disgrace, and injustice. The most important thing is that we still must courageously and boldly maintain our faith in God. What an emotional, psychological and spiritual torture?

The most important thing in the ordeal of Job is that God is not the cause of Job's predicament. Jeremiah 11v:29 says "the thought that I have for you is the thought of good and not evil, to give you an expected end." As human beings, looking at the inexplicable lesson learnt from the story of Job, the end explains the result. It is obvious that we need to start looking further than where we are at the moment of trial. We need to stop limiting God from all He does and all He wants to do in our lives, by thinking for God and wrongly concluding that whatever bad or worse situation we find ourselves is caused by sin. Job's friends who were looking for causes and solutions through their experience searched for answers but were only able to find useless and wrong answers, which made God to rebuke them.

It is human nature to believe that God is punishing us for a sinful act even when the very reason for the predicament is not given. God is limitless, inexhaustible, indefinable, infinite and inexplicable. He never runs out of anything, but bigger and grander than anything in the world. God is abundant in grace, blessing, favour, mercy and salvation!

It does not make sense for someone who releases you from charges to as well be the one to charge you! In the end, God flooded Job's life with blessings, honour, and goodness than he had ever known. Our past cannot be the forecast of our future. If we look for the place of Christ, all we see or get is the structure of who, where, when, and the question is, can we stand in His place? Can we even stand in Job's place? We find it difficult to contemplate the thought of Christ's pierced hands, dripping with the blood of so many innocent and deserving victims. Eventually, Christ illuminates God's nature, and because of Christ, we are no longer in the dark about what God is like, for Christ is the radiance of God's glory, which is full of grace and truth.

Prayer Points

- Father, take me out of the pit of insignificant to into the arena of significance in Jesus name.

- Father, let my life be an environmental transformer in Jesus name.

- Father, show me thy way and let Your presence always go with me in Jesus name.

- Father, break every yoke of stagnancy in my life in Jesus name.

- Father, let the strong man of bad luck troubling my destiny die in Jesus name.

- I withdraw my name from the book of bad luck by the power in the blood of Jesus

- Every bad luck power pursuing my life must be destroyed by the power of the Holy Ghost.

- Father, let the power of the Holy Ghost lift me to where no man can pull me down in Jesus name.

- Every power assigned to turn my glory to shame must be destroyed in Jesus name

- Father, let the windows of opportunity begin to open before me in Jesus name
- Every padlock power assigned to stop me must be broken into pieces in Jesus name.
- Every power delaying my blessing must be uprooted in Jesus name.
- Every buried blessing belonging to me, arise and locate me in Jesus name.
- Every power, working against my favour, your time is up, clear off in Jesus name.
- I enter into greatness by the power in the blood of Jesus.

8

WHAT REALLY DOESN'T MAKE SENSE?

Is it God or human beings? If the table were to be turned and we became Adam, would we not eat of the forbidden fruit? Have you ever asked yourself the question, Who is God? Who are you? How did you find yourself on this planet? Who is Adam and what does Eve look like? Where does the contemporary argument of the problem of evil emerge from? Moreover, how can the problem of evil be solved? We must make conscious effort to stop heaping blames on God for our predicaments, knowing sufficiently well that we are also players in this theatrics of world's inexplicable events.

Though it sounds dumb, we were made to understand from the book of Genesis that even with all the attributes of God being emphasised, we still cannot understand or predict God's behaviour. The first thing that makes God very special is that He is the most significant being in the universe. God creates but was never created! What makes God so great firstly is His Omniscient attribute, which is His all-knowing quality, the completeness of His knowledge. The Bible points out that God knows everything completely and perfectly.

We need to begin to comprehend the sacred reality which must remain an impeccable mystery, though, more than we can bear, but still exerts an endless attraction. Our world appears attractive, beautiful and overwhelming, yet still very disturbing and tragic! A crisis is not what makes a person but shows what a person is made of. What life does to you depends on what life finds in you; the same sun that hardens the clay melts the ice.

Man, not God, is the determining factor of what is right and wrong. Therefore, morality is subject to whatever individual's desire. Man is thereby, responsible only to and for Himself. As human beings, we need to understand the nature of God, even the nature of wisdom, and most importantly, the difference between God's divine wisdom and man's wisdom. God goes beyond speech and description; He is such an experience which fulfils and transfigures humanity without violating its integrity.

What Really Doesn't Make Sense?

Many people lack the divine wisdom of God to interpret and understand situations and circumstances accurately, and therefore the sovereignty of God and His mercy. God is an incontrovertible reality. Even the Greek idea of God, Trinity and incarnation make it difficult for many to comprehend the person of Christ. Divine wisdom matters to us as Christians and children of God as it is rare, priceless and timeless. There is no way we can purchase it as human beings because God possesses it all.

Since the time of Job, human beings have been trying to MAKE SENSE of what goes on around their world, and still, no one has been able to discover the key. We find it hard to predict the weather, not to even mention the dynamics of history, irrespective of the circumstances we find ourselves. Realising the unique truth that, our God is sovereign in all things, is enough for us to be able to face the world and even serve the unstable world. God gave us the right to choose and make decisions in order not to force His decision upon us but remains the Ruler of the whole universe or if otherwise, He overrules, despite our resistance and rebellion. God's will must still prevail. On the contrary, assuming God is not sovereign, one would wonder if freewill will be accorded to human beings. What impression would this then convey to us about

God? He ends up as the Omnipotent that is powerless to control humanity, the Omniscient who is ignorant of human craving, the Omnipresent, benevolent but a killer, wise but unpredictable, fair but biased and preferential.

God surpasses all human imaginations, thoughts and ingenuities. When natural occurrences happen, or there's famine, or starving, suffering, plagues and all sorts, we find it hard as humans, to believe that God in His Omnipotent power is in control of creation. We experience God in diverse ways each day and every day and time that goes by reminds us of God's word and what is written in the Bible from Genesis to Revelation; very insightful, penetrative and sharp-witted. For many of us, it seems like the survival of the fittest, having to struggle to remain physically, morally and spiritually intact. For some of us, we are like the wind that blows, get frustrated and goes away without showing a paradigm shift. When we read the Bible from Genesis to Revelation, we realise the fact that, even the patriarchs experienced a fit of clay and mud.

The director opened the scene with an episode where Adam and Eve must be banished from Eden, a place of unlimited righteousness, peace, joy and eternity. It was then announced that they lost it; they lost the glory which extends to their generation. Thereby the next scene shows mankind in general as being careless, irresponsible, faulty, selfish and spiritless. Noah was said to have struggled with the flood and egotistical like many of us lesser mortals, Abraham came into the scene when God decided to test mankind for their faithfulness in Him. Abraham entertained strangers at Mamre and received blessings from God. Jacob had to wrestle with God and realised that he was struggling with his brother and himself. Joseph must encounter God in prison to end up in the palace, but all seem to no avail. None of them was presented as people who have achieved virtue.

It took God a whole four hundred years of silence - it was the inter-testament period that gave birth to Christianity after God's final message through prophet Malachi after He had paused in His communications through men. It was four hundred years of gross darkness, when nothing was making sense, no prophet, no inspired writer, and for mankind then, the question was "Where is God?" "Does He even care anymore?" Then it seemed that God's silence was not making sense to humanity, but when God did make sense, when the fullness of time came, God sent forth His Son, that was born of a woman, born under the law, so that he might redeem those who were under the law and ultimately that we might receive adoptions as sons. God has sent the spirit of His Son into our hearts, crying, Abba father, therefore, we are no longer slaves, but sons, and if sons, then heirs through God.

When God does make sense, human beings then must also show some sense of responsibility, so that we can achieve the integration and the entire unity that we desire by acknowledging our flaws, comply with our natures, crimes, sadness, despair and bitterness. For God to make sense to us, we must be willing and ready to make peace with the past and to the best of our knowledge. Though it seems like a struggle between David and Goliath, history has it that, those who know their God shall do great exploits. Consequently, if we commit ourselves to the struggle or responsibility, everything around us including God will begin to make sense.

BIBLIOGRAPHY

1. Accad, Fouad. Elias, Building Bridges: Christianity and Islam (Colorado Springs, CO: NavPress, 1997).

2. Adeyemo, Tokunboh, Africa Bible Commentary: A One-Volume Commentary Written by 70 African Scholars (Nairobi, Kenya: WordAlive Publishers, 2006).

3. Armstrong, Karen, A History of God: From Abraham to the Present: The 4000-Year Quest for God (London, GB: Vintage, 1999).

4. Armstrong, Karen, In the Beginning: A New Interpretation of Genesis (London, GB: Vintage, 2011).

5. Bloom J. (2014): When God seems silent: https://www.desiringgod.org/articles/when-god-seems-silent. Accessed 10th March 2018.

6. Carter, Tom, 13 Crucial Questions Jesus Wants to Ask You: (Sabo, Yaba, Lagos: Kregel Publications, 1999).

7. Dobson, Dr James, When God doesn't make sense: (Wheaton, IL: Tyndale House Publishers, 2012).

8. Ford, David F, Shaping Theology: Engagements in a Religious and Secular World (Oxford, UK: Blackwell Publishing, 2007).

9. Gill, Robin, Christian Ethics: Second Edition (Cambridge, UK: Cambridge University Press, 2012).

10. MacArthur, John, The Macarthur Study Bible: Revised and Updated Large Print Edition (Nashville, TN: Thomas Nelson Inc, 1980).

11. Maiden, Peter, Discipleship: (Crownhill, MK: Authentic Media Limited, 2011).

12. Peterson, Eugene H, Subversive Spirituality: (Cambridge, UK: WBE Publishing Company, 1997).

13. Meyer, F. B, The Life of Joseph: Beloved, Hated and Exalted (Lynnwood, WA: Emerald Books, 1995).

14. Story, Dan, Defending Your Faith: Reliable Answer for a New Generation of Seekers and Skeptics (Grand Rapids, MI: Kregel Publications, 1997).

15. Thorp, Helen, Developing Our Pastoral Wisdom: Reflecting Together on Pastoral Care (Cambridge, UK: Grove Books Limited, 2013).

16. Warren, Rick, The Purpose Driven Life: (Zondervan, Grand Rapids, Michigan, 2002).

17. Wiersbe, Warren W, Be responsible: Being Good Stewards of God's Gift (Colorado Springs, CO: David C Cook Publishing Company, 2002).

18. Wright, N Tom, Who was Jesus?: (London, GB: SPCK, 1992).

19. Rundle, Elizabeth, Joseph: The Power of Forgiveness and Reconciliation (Farnham, UK: CWR, 2003).

20. Frame, John M, Apologetics to the Glory of God: An Introduction (Phillipsburg, NJ: P&R Publishing, 1994).

21. Kenneth, Okey, Propellers of Academic Success: What You Need to Know To Excel In Your Studies (Lagos, NGR: Zentex Ventures, 2011).

www.ingramcontent.com/pod-product-compliance
Lightning Source LLC
Chambersburg PA
CBHW071312060426
42444CB00034B/1959